Thor
HEYERDAHL

Thor
HEYERDAHL

by John Malam

Carolrhoda Books, Inc. / Minneapolis

Carolrhoda Books, Inc., c/o The Lerner Publishing Group
241 First Avenue North, Minneapolis, Minnesota 55401 U.S.A.

Website address: www.lernerbooks.com

Library of Congress Cataloging-in-Publication Data

Malam, John.
  Thor Heyerdahl / John Malam.
     p.   cm. — (Tell me about)
  Includes index.
  Summary: A biography of the Norwegian explorer whose voyages were
undertaken to prove certain theories about the migration patterns of
ancient people.
  ISBN 1–57505–364–0 (alk. paper)
  1. Heyerdahl, Thor—Juvenile literature. 2. Explorers—Norway—
Biography—Juvenile literature. [1. Heyerdahl, Thor.
2. Explorers.] I. Title. II. Series: Tell me about (Minneapolis, Minn.)
G306.H47M35 1999
910'.4—dc21   98–8487

Printed by Graficas Reunidas SA, Spain
Bound in the United States of America
1 2 3 4 5 6 – OS – 04 03 02 01 00 99

Thor Heyerdahl is a famous explorer from Norway. For most of his life, he has wanted to find out about people from long ago. He thinks some of them might have sailed across the world's oceans to look for new lands. To see if his ideas could be right, he has gone on exciting journeys. This is his story.

Thor Heyerdahl

Thor Heyerdahl was born in 1914, in Larvik, a small fishing town in southern Norway.

When he was a boy, Thor liked to explore the world around him. He walked along the coast and through the countryside. He collected seashells, butterflies, and animals. Once he even brought home a poisonous snake!

(Left) Thor learned to ski when he was young. In this photo, he is four years old.

(Right) Thor's house in Larvik, Norway

Every summer, Thor and his mother went to the mountains for a vacation. They liked to walk across the moors.

On one of their walks, they met a man called Ola Bjorneby. Ola lived all alone on the wild moors. He lived a simple life. There was something that Thor liked about the way Ola lived. When Thor was fourteen, he spent the summer as Ola's helper.

Thor liked walking on Norway's wild moors.

Back at home in Larvik, Thor wondered if he could live a simple life, too, just like Ola. He read about the tiny islands in the Pacific Ocean, on the other side of the world.

Thor and his friend Arthur Jacoby often talked about the islands. They wondered what it would be like to live there.

Thor dreamed of living on a small Pacific island like this one.

When he was old enough, Thor went to Oslo University and studied many kinds of science. His teacher said that he should live on a Pacific island and study how animals had crossed the sea to get there.

Liv Torp was also a student at the university. She wanted to live on an island, too. Thor and Liv were married on Christmas Eve, 1936. On Christmas Day they set off on their island adventure.

Oslo, the capital of Norway, where Thor was a student

Thor and Liv sailed to Fatu Hiva. It was a beautiful island in the South Pacific. It was so far away that it took more than nine weeks to get there.

Fatu Hiva was very different from Norway. There were no cars or trains, and no electricity.

Life on the island was simpler than in Norway. Thor and Liv picked oranges, mangoes, and coconuts, and they caught fish to eat.

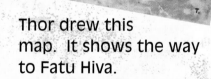

Thor drew this map. It shows the way to Fatu Hiva.

All these fruits grow on Pacific islands.

Thor made friends with people on the island. Tioti showed Thor an old carved model of a strange-looking boat. Tei-Tetua told Thor a story about how the people first came to Fatu Hiva. He said a god named Kon-Tiki had brought them across the sea from a land far away. He pointed toward South America.

One of Thor and Liv's homes on Fatu Hiva

Thor and Liv stayed on Fatu Hiva for a year. Then they went home to Norway.

The boat carving, the story about the god Kon-Tiki, and Thor's studies of the ocean gave him an idea. In those days, experts thought the first people to live on the Pacific islands had come from Asia. But Thor believed they had sailed from South America. He set out to show how this was possible.

Thor at home in Norway

Thor knew that long ago the people who lived in South America had made rafts of balsa wood. He went to South America and built a big raft from balsa wood, bamboo, reeds, and leaves. He called it *Kon-Tiki,* after the god in Tei-Tetua's story.

On April 27, 1947, the *Kon-Tiki* sailed from Peru, in South America. On board were Thor and five of his friends.

Thor used bamboo *(left)* and balsa wood to build the *Kon-Tiki (below)*. Many people thought the raft would sink.

Thor and his crew caught sharks during the *Kon-Tiki's* voyage.

The *Kon-Tiki* bobbed up and down like a cork. It did not sink. The wind and the ocean's current carried the raft far across the Pacific Ocean.

After 101 days, the *Kon-Tiki* landed on a Pacific island. Thor had shown that people from South America could have sailed to the Pacific islands long ago.

Thor and the *Kon-Tiki* became famous. But not everyone believed his idea.

Thor sailed the *Kon-Tiki* across more than four thousand miles of dangerous ocean.

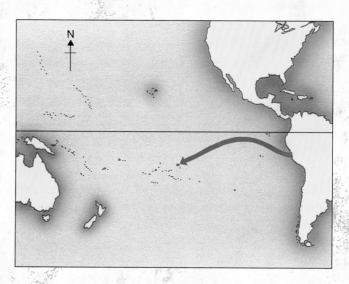

Thor looks at the kneeling statue on Easter Island.

In October 1955 Thor traveled to Easter Island in the South Pacific. There he saw the island's huge, mysterious stone statues. One showed a kneeling man. It reminded him of ancient statues from Peru, in South America.

Thor thought the presence of this statue helped prove that the first Pacific islanders had come from South America. He hoped it would convince other people.

15

Thor's next adventure, in 1961, was when he sailed across the Atlantic Ocean. He wanted to find out if people long ago could have sailed from Africa to America. Thor wondered about this because he had seen ancient Egyptian paintings of reed boats. The boats were like some pictured on ceramic pots in Peru. Perhaps people sailed from Africa in reed boats. For his journey, Thor built a boat made out of reeds.

People in South America still make boats out of reeds.

The reed boat *Ra II*, in which Thor
crossed the Atlantic Ocean

Thor called his reed boat *Ra,* after the ancient
Egyptian sun god. Thor's first boat was damaged by
storms. He built another one, called *Ra II.* He set
out from Morocco, in Africa. After fifty-seven days
at sea, he reached the West Indies, near South
America.

Once again, Thor had shown that ancient people
could have sailed across the world's oceans.

Thor's last sea adventure was in a reed boat called *Tigris*. He sailed it across the Indian Ocean and landed in the country of Djibouti, in Africa.

Building the *Tigris*

Thor could land only in Djibouti because the countries near it were troubled by war and hunger. These things made Thor feel sad and angry. He decided to do something to show how upset he was.

Thor set fire to the *Tigris* in Djibouti's harbor. Then he sent a letter to the United Nations to say that all countries of the world should work toward peace. Otherwise, he said, our world would be turned into a sinking ship, just like the *Tigris*.

The *Tigris* in flames

Thor Heyerdahl has spent his life exploring the world's mysteries. He believes the people of the past were explorers too, crossing the seas to find new lands. His adventures have tried to show how much of the world those people might have seen.

The boats that Thor Heyerdahl used on his adventures are as famous as he is. The *Kon-Tiki* and *Ra II* are kept in a special museum in Oslo, Norway.

Many people visit the Kon-Tiki museum, where Thor's boats are kept.

Important Dates

1914 Thor Heyerdahl was born in Norway

1937-1938 Lived for a year on Fatu Hiva

1947 Sailed the *Kon-Tiki* across the Pacific Ocean

1955 Led an expedition to Easter Island

1969 *Ra I* sank in the Atlantic Ocean

1970 Sailed *Ra II* across the Atlantic Ocean

1977-1978 Sailed the *Tigris* across the Indian Ocean

1982-1984 Worked in the Maldives, a group of islands in the Indian Ocean

1986-1988 Worked on Easter Island again

Thor wearing an ancient crown, on Fatu Hiva

Key Words

balsa
a light wood that floats well

moors
areas of rolling, often watery lands

papyrus
a type of tall reed

raft
a bundle of logs or other pieces of wood tied together and used for floating on water

Index

Acknowledgments

The author and publisher gratefully acknowledge the following for permission to reproduce copyrighted material:
Cover The Kon-Tiki Museum, Oslo, Norway
Title page Johnathan T Wright/Bruce Coleman Limited
page 5 The Kon-Tiki Museum, Oslo, Norway **page 6** (left) The Kon-Tiki Museum, Oslo, Norway (right) The Larvik Tourist Board **page 7** Janos Jurka/Bruce Coleman Limited **page 8** L Isy-Schwart/Image Bank **page 9** Thomas Buchholz/Bruce Coleman Limited **page 10** (left) Du Boisberran/Image Bank (right) The Kon-Tiki Museum, Oslo, Norway **page 11** The Kon-Tiki Museum, Oslo, Norway **page 12** The Kon-Tiki Museum, Oslo, Norway **page 13** (left) Granville Harris/Bruce Coleman Limited (right) The Kon-Tiki Museum, Oslo, Norway **page 14** The Kon-Tiki Museum, Oslo, Norway **page 15** The Kon-Tiki Museum, Oslo, Norway **page 16** The Kon-Tiki Museum, Oslo, Norway **page 17** The Kon-Tiki Museum, Oslo, Norway **page 18** (both) Johnathan T Wright/Bruce Coleman Limited **page 19** The Kon-Tiki Museum, Oslo, Norway **page 20** The Kon-Tiki Museum, Oslo, Norway **page 21** The Kon-Tiki Museum, Oslo, Norway

About the Author

John Malam has a degree in ancient history and archeology from the University of Birmingham in England. He is the author of many children's books on topics that include history, natural history, natural science, and biography. Before becoming a writer and editor, he directed archeological excavations. Malam lives in Manchester, England, with his wife, Hilary, and their children, Joseph and Eve.